FOURTH ESTATE PRESENTS   BRYAN LEE O'MALLEY

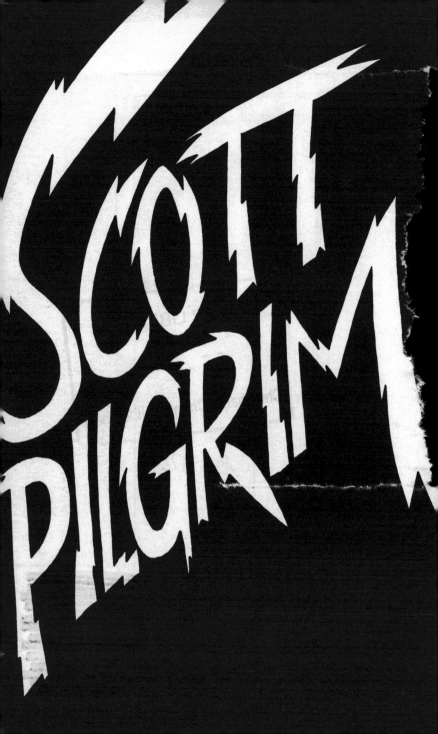

IN HIS FINEST HOUR

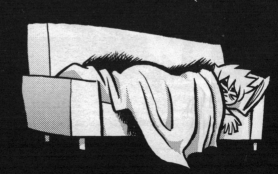

John Kantz art assistant
Aaron Ancheta junior assistant
Ben Berntsen back cover art
Dylan McCrae cover colors
Bryan Lee O'Malley and **Keith Wood** book design
James Lucas Jones editor

This production 2012
ISBN: 978-0-00-793084-5

First published in Great Britain in 2010 by
Fourth Estate
An imprint of HarperCollins*Publishers*
77–85 Fulham Palace Road
London W6 8JB
www.4thestate.co.uk

Simultaneously published in the United States by Oni Press

Printed in Great Britain by Clays Ltd, St Ives plc

Things stop happening

32

I DON'T WANT SEX! NOT EVERYTHING IS ABOUT SEX!

YOU NEED TO MOVE ON, SCOTT. SOME HOT DOUCHEY GUY STOLE YOUR GIRLFRIEND. *FORGET HER.* GET *OVER IT.*

I'M OVER IT.

OE BRAND mac n cheez

WE DON'T *KNOW* HE STOLE HER. SHE JUST... HASN'T COME BACK! YET.

OVER IT.

ANYWAY, I *HAVE* MOVED ON!

LOOK AT THIS BRAND NEW GAMING DEVICE YOUNG NEIL GAVE ME! IT'S LIKE THE HOTTEST, NEWEST, HOTTEST THING!

SOME OTHER NIGHT

REMEMBER HOW YOU BROKE YOUR BASS? LIKE... 4 MONTHS AGO?

I DON'T THINK IT WAS 4 *MONTHS* AGO.

ANYWAY, WE'RE PLAYING AT CAMERON HOUSE ON MONDAY, AND, I MEAN, YOU COULD COME.

...SCOTT.

OH DUDE, I FINALLY BEAT THIS— THIS ONE GUY...

I BEAT THIS ONE GUY... VIDEO GAMES...

16

DOES THAT MEAN YOU WERE PRACTICALLY SIXTEEN WHEN WE MET?

NO WAY! WE MET ON MY SEVENTEENTH BIRTHDAY, SILLY!

SKOOCH SKOOCH

SO... UH... HOW'S IT FEEL TO BE... UH... NO LONGER A CHILD IN THE EYES OF THE LAW?

SKETCHY-ASS 24-YEAR-OLD

AW... IT'S OKAY.

BUH?

I'M MOVING *AWAY* SOON! I APPLIED TO MCGILL AND UBC AND I'M GRADUATING IN *THREE MONTHS!!!*

SO THAT HAPPENED.

I'M TRULY FLATTERED BY YOUR DELIGHTFUL OFFER, BUT LET'S TRY TO BE *GROWNUPS* HERE, OKAY?

IT'S WALLACE'S FAULT! HE GAVE ME CONFUSING ADVICE! HOW I HATE HIM.

YEAH... SCOTT, DO YOU REMEMBER HOW YOU, LIKE, CHEATED ON ME AND STUFF? KIND OF A CRUMMY BOYFRIEND, IN RETROSPECT?

scotty ur so hot & sexxy

o hey thanx

I... UHH... SORT OF...

MEMORY CAM

SCOTT, I DON'T *WANT* YOU ANYMORE.

IT DOESN'T MEAN I DON'T *LOVE* YOU.

BUT... I'VE MOVED ON.

YOU LIKE STEPHEN STILLS, DON'T YOU?

STEPHEN? PSSH HAHA HAHA

WHY IS THAT FUNNY?

I'M HAPPY BEING ALONE RIGHT NOW, SCOTT. I'M TRYING TO LEARN TO LIKE *ME. ALONE.*

I MEAN, I'VE SPENT A YEAR OF MY LIFE ON YOU!

...IT'S COOL IF WE JUST MAKE OUT FOR A WHILE.

SMOOCH

BUT IT WAS HORRIBLE

FOR **EVERYONE**

AND THAT INCLUDES YOU

33 She says what she means

WHERE YOU BEEN? I DIDN'T KNOW YOU KNEW SARAH JANE.

WHO THE HELL IS SARAH JANE?

THIS IS HER PARTY, MAN.

IT'S HER BIRTHDAY.

...WHAT AM I DOING HERE?

I THOUGHT THIS WAS A JULIE PARTY.

JULIE MOVED TO MONTREAL.

YOUNG NEIL (NOT REALLY VERY YOUNG)

WHAT?!

I HEARD ENVY ADAMS WAS HERE.

ENVY ADAMS? NO WAY!

APPARENTLY SHE LOOKS AMAZING.

OH MAN! I'M TOTALLY GAY FOR HER.

MONIQUE AGAIN?

SANDRA LIKE, WHAT THE HELL

WHAT THE HELL, YOUNG NEIL, IS THIS TRUE?

SHE DOES LOOK AMAZING. YOU SHOULD JUST, LIKE, PREEMPTIVELY BE A DICK TO HER, MAN.

REALLY? THAT WORKS?

ENVY ADAMS? PARTYING WITH *MERE* MORTALS?

WHIP

WHY DON'T YOU GO BACK TO...

TO...

MONTREALHALLA

WE'LL SPARE YOU THE EMBARRASSMENT OF WITNESSING THE REST OF THIS AWFUL SPECTACLE.

(TURN THE PAGE)

VERY MATURE, SCOTT.

LIKE YOU ACTUALLY CARE.

OF COURSE I CARE. DON'T BE A BABY.

POUT

YOU MAKE ME OUT TO BE SOME KIND OF *VILLAINESS*. WE WERE PRACTICALLY *KIDS* WHEN WE DATED, SCOTT, AND IT'S NOT LIKE *YOU* WERE SOME PARAGON OF VIRTUE.

I WAS *SUCH* A PARAGON.

CHUG

AND.

I WAS *SUCH* A PARAGON!

OVER IT.

WHAT IS THE *DEAL* WITH HER, MAN?? I SWEAR TO GOD!! SHE'S GOT SINISTER MOTIVES OR SOMETHING! GIDEON SENT HER TO MESS WITH MY HEAD!!

SHE'S THE DEVIL, SCOTT.

(HE HAD COFFEE)

GIDEON'S PROBABLY IN TOWN, TOO! THEY'RE IN *CAHOOTS*, MAN!! WHAT THE HELL DO I *DO*??

OF COURSE HE'S IN TOWN. DIDN'T YOU READ THE ARTICLE I SHOWED YOU?

OH MAN! MAYBE SHE WANTS TO GET BACK TOGETHER!

PSSH. SHE'S SCREWING GIDEON, OBVIOUSLY.

45

HM...

NO, RAMONA'S SCREWING GIDEON...

WELL, THE THREE OF THEM CAN ALL SCREW, CAN'T THEY?

SO LIKE, ME AND ENVY ARE LIKE 24 NOW, RIGHT?

SHE'S 25. HER BIRTHDAY WAS IN FEBRUARY.

WHAT? HOW DO YOU KNOW?

IT WAS A BIG DEAL, GUY.

I READ ABOUT THE PARTY IN ITALIAN *VOGUE*. I THINK DAVID BOWIE WAS THERE.

OK, BUT WE'RE GROWING UP A BIT, RIGHT?? WE'RE MOVING ON!!

MOVING ON TO THREE-SOMES WITH GIDEON AND RAMONA.

SALE! TAKE OUR BOOKS-THEIR...

AND THEN WALLACE BOUGHT HIM SUSHI.

MM! IT'S GOOD!

46

THAT NIGHT

ONE NEW MESSAGE.

4:18 PM.

WHUMP

HEY, IT'S KIM.

↑ON

I JUST SAW A GUY WITH A PARKA EXACTLY LIKE YOUR STUPID PARKA YOU'VE HAD SINCE YOU WERE 12.

THAT'S LITERALLY THE MOST INTERESTING THING THAT'S HAPPENED ALL WEEK. IT FRIGGIN' SUCKS UP HERE.

GET OVER YOUR EXTREMELY BORING DEPRESSION AND COME VISIT ME SOMETIME, ASS-CLOWN.

CLICK

47

THE
NEXT
DAY...

49

WE WENT BOWLING AT MIDNIGHT. JULIE AND STEPHEN BAKED ME A TERRIBLE CAKE.

YOU GOT PRETTY DRUNK.

I DON'T DRINK.

MM-HMM.

SO DO YOU THINK WE'RE GOING TO GET BACK TOGETHER?

HUH? WHAT, ME AND YOU?

OR MAYBE JUST HAVE *CASUAL SEX?*

• • • •

51

I SEE YOU FINALLY GOT SOME SLEEP.

WHAT ARE YOU, PSYCHIC?

SCOTT, WE DATED FOR TWO YEARS.

I CAN READ YOU LIKE A BOOK.

TWO YEARS?

YOU DON'T EVEN *REMEMBER* ME.

YOU'RE, LIKE, THE ONLY ONE WHO KNEW ME *BEFORE...*

BEFORE WHAT?

SCOTT, DO YOU REMEMBER *ANYTHING?*

LIKE, *EVER?*

— omigod ur like, such a stud

yeah totes

STUFF.

MEMORY CAM

WHAT ABOUT NEW YEAR'S EVE? DO YOU REMEMBER THAT?

WE HAD A FIGHT.

LIKE A *FIGHT* FIGHT?

A FIGHT THAT *YOU* STARTED.

WELL, I REMEMBER YOU *BREAKING MY HEART.*

THE FEELING IS SOMEWHAT MUTUAL.

I KNOW I'M CHANGING. WE'RE ALL CHANGING.

JUST... DON'T FORGET ME.

THIS IS THE ONLY ME *HE* KNOWS...

YOU NEED TO FACE REALITY, SCOTT.

HE'S NOT EVEN A BAD *GUY*.

DUNDAS STREET COACH TERMINAL

THE GREAT WHITE NORTH

58

34 A link to the past

I MEAN, ARE YOU GOING TO SCHOOL, OR...?

GLARE

WAIT, WHAT IS THIS? WHERE ARE WE GOING?

YOU WANT A WILDERNESS SABBATICAL, YOU'RE GONNA GET THE REAL THING.

THANKS FOR COMING.

I'VE BEEN GOING A LITTLE BIT CRAZY UP HERE.

WHAT ARE YOU *DOING* HERE, KIM?

I'LL LET YOU KNOW WHEN I FIGURE IT OUT.

NOT TO MENTION YOU SCREWED OVER POOR SIMON LEE...

...WELL, WE BOTH DID, BUT THE LOOK ON HIS FACE...

RUB RUB

THIS IS THE BEST ST JOEL'S COULD MUSTER?

SIMON LEE?

BUT... HE WAS A BAD GUY.

SIMON LEE? THE CHINESE KID?

I WAS DATING HIM, SCOTT. I MEAN, I THINK HE HUGGED ME ONCE.

YOU'RE GOING DOWN, SIMON!!

SIMON

AND IT'LL NEVER HAPPEN AGAIN.

SCOTT PILGRIM IS COMING HOME...

Toronto 80

...AND THIS TIME, IT'S PERSONAL!!

MMM... I DUNNO.

MAYBE LOSE THE SHOULDERS.

GIDEON GRAVES
(31 YEARS OLD)

OCCUPATION:
ASSHOLE

I WANT SOME OPTIONS ON THE SHOES.

AND HAIR, PEOPLE, MY *GOD* *PLEASE.* I WANT YOU TO BUILD A BONFIRE IN HER HAIR. THAT IS A METAPHOR.

BACKSTAGE

GIDEON, CAN WE TALK?

WALK WITH ME, BABY.

I'VE GOT LIGHTING TO REVIEW AND I NEED TO DO MY THIRD-TO-LAST WALKTHROUGH. DOORS IN... WHAT?

104 MINUTES!

104 AND COUNTING, ENVY, HONEY, YOU KNOW I LOVE YOU. WHAT'S ON YOUR MIND?

I'M JUST *TIRED!* I'VE BEEN TRAINING AND LEARNING CHOREOGRAPHY FOR *WEEKS.* I'VE TRIED ON 71 DRESSES.

CAN'T WE JUST SIT DOWN FOR AN HOUR AND HAVE A DRINK? THE OUTFIT IS *FINE.* I'M *READY.*

NATALIE. IT'S YOUR *DEBUT.*

IT'S THE OPENING OF MY SPECIAL PLACE IN TORONTO. YOUR OUTFIT IS *IMPORTANT.*

I'VE HAD SOME VERY PROMISING YOUNG DESIGNERS *LITERALLY* CHAINED TO SEWING MACHINES FOR A MONTH.

AND YOU *KNOW* THAT DRESSING YOU UP LIKE A DOLL IS VERY FULFILLING FOR ME SEXUALLY.

SEEMS LIKE IT'S ABOUT THE *ONLY* THING.

WHAT WAS THAT?

NOTHING.

CHAOS THEATRE
TORONTO

HAVE YOU SEEN HIM?

GRAVES? NOT AT ALL. BUT HE'S DEFINITELY HERE.

THIS PLACE *REEKS* OF A PERSONAL TOUCH.

WHO ARE WE TALKING ABOUT?

OTHER SCOTT, HAVE YOU SEEN RAMONA?

IS SHE THE ONE WITH THE GLASSES, OR THE ONE WITH THE FRECKLES?

...NEVER MIND.

TAKE OFF YOUR JACKET, GUY! STAY A WHILE!

THIS CLUB HAS GIRLS, TOO!

ZZZIP

IT'S SEVEN DOLLARS, JOSEPH. I'LL HOLD MY COAT.

QUIT ACTING LIKE A BROKE-ASS BITCH.

COAT CHEC

GIVE ME SOMETHING WITH ICE IN IT. AND BOOZE.

BOOZE AND ICE, PLEASE.

GRIP

SIP

I... JULIE... YOU... I... MONTREAL...

UHH...

YOU'RE A MESS, MAN. WOULD YOU LOOK AT YOURSELF?

DURR?

WHYYYYYY

HEY.

I GOT A FEW OF THESE LEFT. VIRAL MARKETING.

SAD.

NICE SHIRT, SCOTT!

STACEY PILGRIM
(LONG-SUFFERING YOUNGER SISTER)

SHUT UP. I SPILLED MY DRINK.

HAVE YOU SEEN RAMONA?

THE RAMONA WHO BROKE YOUR HEART AND RUINED YOUR LIFE AND HAD A THREESOME WITH THIS GIDEON CLOWN?

YOU NEED TO STOP TALKING TO WALLACE, OKAY?

ANYWAY, I THOUGHT YOU DIDN'T DRINK!!!

TIME CRITICS

OH... HEY, MAN.

UH-HUH.

PEW PEW

YOUNG NEIL

PEW

WAIT, DO YOU TWO NOT KNOW EACH OTHER? THAT'S CRAZY!

NUH-UH.

SCOTT'S SISTER, RIGHT?

PEW PEW

YEAH, HI.

STACEY, THIS IS YOUNG—

—THIS IS, UM, NEIL.

NEIL

This is the greatest day of his life.

ANYWAY.

SCOTT! HEY!

NICE SHIRT!

KNIVES (18 YEARS OLD)

TAMARA (HER BEST FRIEND)

UH... YEAH. HOW'S IT GOING?

GREAT!

AWESOME!!

HEY, HAVE YOU GUYS SEEN—

YES!! I TOTALLY SAW ENVY ADAMS!! I MEAN I THINK I DID! IT LOOKED JUST LIKE HER!!

DID YOU LIKE HER SOLO ALBUM?

AREN'T WE AT THE RELEASE PARTY FOR IT?

PLEASE, IT LEAKED MONTHS AGO.

OH...

I HAVEN'T SEEN RAMONA, OR GIDEON GRAVES, OR—

KACHUNK

EEEEEE!!!

SCOTT!
WATCH OUT!
I THINK
THAT GUY
MIGHT BE
GIDEON!

YOU'RE GIDEON?

SCOTT PILGRIM. CAN I JUST BE THE FIRST TO SAY... NICE SHIRT.

WHAT?

SHUT UP! YOU'RE LIKE THE THIRD PERSON TO SAY THAT!

I HAVEN'T LAID A FINGER ON HER, AMIGO. SHE'S PROBABLY IN THE LADIES' ROOM.

WHAT? *RAMONA*, DUDE.

WAIT, WHAT?

YOU...

YOU DON'T HAVE HER?

...SHE ISN'T WITH *YOU?*

PUMMEL

I PLANNED THIS THROUGH TO THE END ASSUMING YOU'D AT LEAST BE *COMPETENT* ENOUGH TO *KEEP HER AROUND!*

YOU DEFEATED *SIX* OF HER EVIL EX-BOYFRIENDS AND SHE *LEFT* YOU?!

SHUT UP! IT'S COMPLICATED!

IT'S *QUITE SIMPLE,* ACTUALLY!

THAT MAKES YOU THE NEWEST MEMBER OF THE *LEAGUE,* DOESN'T IT?

THE LEAGUE OF EVIL EX-BOY-FRIENDS?

JOIN ME, SCOTT, AND I WILL COMPLETE YOUR TRAINING! TOGETHER WE CAN *RULE* RAMONA'S FUTURE LOVE LIFE!

I'LL NEVER JOIN YOU!!!

WUMP

DEAD

129

WELL, AT LEAST YOU WEREN'T WITH *HIM*.

GIDEON, I MEAN.

THAT ASS.

I'M SORRY.

I'M SORRY I LEFT. THOSE LAST FEW DAYS... I WAS PRETTY MESSED UP.

I DIDN'T WANT YOU TO GET MESSED UP TOO.

I GOT KINDA MESSED UP ANYWAY.

BUT... YOU'RE SO *TOUGH*.

134

I CAME BACK FOR *ME*, SCOTT. I CAME BACK TO MAKE MYSELF SAY IT.

I CAME BACK TO LOOK YOU IN THE EYES, AND... AND TO ADMIT THAT—

KISS

...TO ADMIT THAT I WAS A CRUMMY GIRLFRIEND AND I FEEL LIKE AN IDIOT FOR EVEN TRYING TO—

138

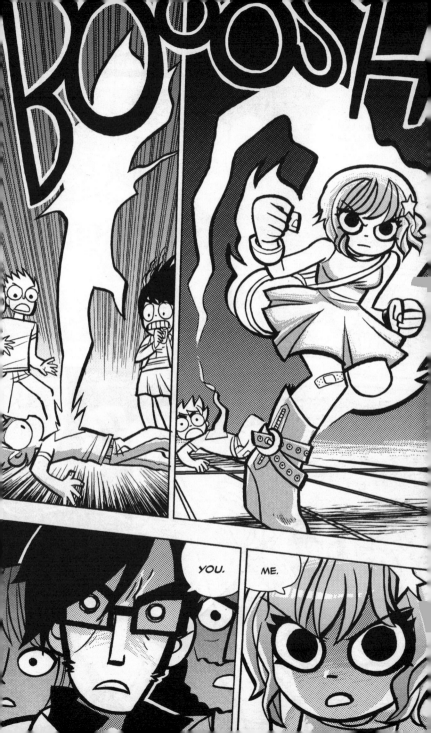

the beginning

YOU'RE NOT FROM AROUND HERE.

YOUR EYES...

THEY'VE SEEN THINGS.

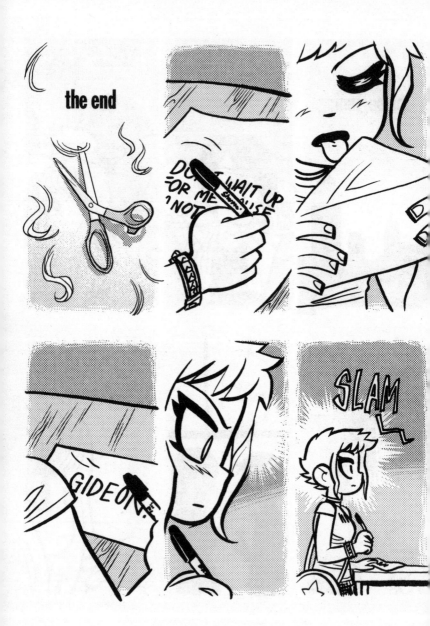

162

YOU IDIOT.
I'M ALL-POWERFUL IN HER HEAD, MAN!
DID YOU THINK I'D JUST ROLL OVER IN HERE?

THUNK

Music sounds better with you 38

...AND NOW I HAVE TO KILL YOU.

LEYEL UP!

GUTS +1
HEART +3
BALLS +2

208

shimmer

OUCH! OOF!
OW! OW! AGH!
AGH! OUCH! UGH!
UNGH! AGH! ARF! YAG
OWCH!

209

CLOSURE

OH, MAN. WERE YOU AND GIDEON, LIKE, A THING?

WE COULD HAVE BEEN, BUT I DOUBT HE EVER FELT THAT WAY.

MAYBE I WAS JUST AFTER THE POWER, THE CONNECTIONS, THE MONEY...

THE MONEY...

ANYWAY, TURNS OUT HE WAS CRAP. I'M OVER IT.

P.S.- GET OFF MY STAGE.

GIMME A COLD ONE. ...OH MY GOD, THE IRONY, RIGHT?

I'VE BEEN IN A *TUBE* SINCE *2003*, MOM, OKAY?

SERIOUSLY. WHY AM I WEARING THIS STUPID DRESS?

SHOULD WE BE PICKING THIS STUFF UP?

SO NOT INTERESTED.

SHRUG

I WAS LOOKING FOR AN EXCUSE TO GET A NEW BAG, ANYWAY.

HEY, CONGRATS, KIDS.

THEY'RE SHUTTING DOWN MY NEW FAVOURITE CLUB AFTER ONE NIGHT BUT I'M GLAD YOU GOT YOUR CRAP SORTED OUT.

SO LIKE, WHEN YOU GUYS DISAPPEARED IN THE MIDDLE OF THE FIGHT... WHAT WAS THAT ALL ABOUT?

OH *MAN!* WE WENT IN RAMONA'S HEAD WHERE GIDEON WAS LIKE EIGHTY FEET TALL AND HOLDING HER PRISONER LIKE A TOTAL BAD DUDE!

THEN I HEADBUTTED HIM AND GAVE HIM THE GLOW AND THEN WERE A MILLION RAMONAS AND THEY KICKED HIS ASS! IT WAS *AMAZING!*

SO WHERE'VE YOU *BEEN* ALL YEAR, RAMMY?

...Y, SHE DOESN'T HAVE ANYTHING TO PROVE...

YOU REALLY WANT TO KNOW?

YES.

DUH, YEAH.

VERY MUCH SO.

M-ME TOO?

I'M A LITTLE CURIOUS, SURE.

DUDES, I JUST WENT TO MY DAD'S.

HE LIVES IN THE MIDDLE OF NOWHERE. I THOUGHT I'D GET MY HEAD TOGETHER AND COME BACK IN A WEEK OR TWO.

YOU KNOW, LIKE A WILDERNESS SABBATICAL.

YOU SEE, SCOTT WILDERNESS

220

YEAH, BUT IT DIDN'T REALLY WORK THAT WAY.

I JUST ENDED UP SLEEPING ALL DAY, DICKING AROUND ON THE INTERNET AND WATCHING EVERY EPISODE OF THE X-FILES. I MEAN, I *TRIED* CALLING YOU, SCOTT...

...YEAH...

...MAYBE YOU TWO WERE MEANT TO BE.

JUST CALL ME FOR THE WEDDING.

222

I GUESS THAT'S MY PROBLEM— I'M ALWAYS TRYING TO BEAT THE CLOCK, OUTRUN THE UNIVERSE...

LIKE NOTHING CAN CHANGE ME, AS LONG AS *I* CHANGE *FIRST*.

I FEEL LIKE I'M IN THIS RIVER, JUST GETTING SWEPT ALONG... AND IF I HOLD ON TO ANYONE, IF I'M HOLDING ON FOR DEAR LIFE, I'M NOT *GETTING* ANYWHERE. I'M STUCK.

...I NEVER WANTED TO GET STUCK.

SO
ANYWAY

YOU WANT TO GRAB A DRINK WITH US AND CHAT?

FREAKING OUT A LOT

I—I'M FREAKING OUT A LITTLE!

OKAY, YEAH, UH, I GUESS I'M GAY. I REALIZED I LIKE DUDES.

IT SHOCKED EVERYONE WHEN I CAME OUT, BACK IN VOLUME 5. YOU SEEMED BUSY, SO I DIDN'T MENTION IT.

SO LIKE... *JULIE* TURNED YOU *GAY?!*

SERIOUSLY. GET NEW ONES.

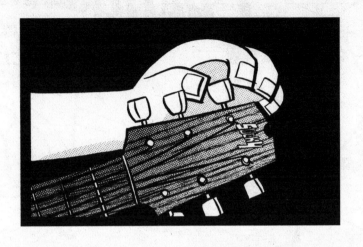

CRITICAL NOTICES

YOU GUYS ARE, UM...

YOU GUYS HAVE SO MUCH POTENTIAL!

THAT WAS AN EXTREMELY BAD COVER OF "I'M A BELIEVER" BY THE MONKEES.

BAD NEWS, SCOTT. THE ONLY TWO PEOPLE WHO COULD EVER BE OUR FANS HAVE DEVELOPED *TASTE*.

HELL, WHO NEEDS 'EM?

WE'LL JUST KEEP PLAYING TO YOUR CAT.

WANT TO DO IT AGAIN?

LET'S DO IT AGAIN.

THEN.

SO UM

I MEAN I GUESS I'LL

snff

BAWL

GIVE ME A CALL WHEN YOU'RE IN TOWN, OKAY?

SCOTT...

YOU'LL ALWAYS BE MY CLASH AT DEMONHEAD.

Whatever that means.

CREATED BY

BRYAN LEE O'MALLEY
(CREATOR — 31 YEARS OLD)

Wrote and drew the book, despite everything.

This book and all the others and the past six years and the other years are all dedicated to Hope Larson.

Thank you and goodnight.

Albums that got me through this:
The Cardigans - *Super Extra Gravity;* Annie - *Don't Stop;*
Neko Case - *Middle Cyclone;* Gorillaz - *Plastic Beach;*
LCD Soundsystem - *This Is Happening;* Sleigh Bells - *Treats;*
Pavement - *Quarantine the Past;* and Spoon - *Transference.*

JOHN KANTZ
Screentone, background art (28 years old)
Artist, Legends From Darkwood.
Designed Gideon's cryogenic apparatus.
www.jackmo.com

AARON ANCHETA
Crowd scenes, inking assist (20 years old)
Student at the University of Arizona. This
is his first published work. Drew a lot of
Ramonas. www.aancheta.com